What I
Believe
Happened

Dr. Gus N. Daisey

Dr. Gus N. Daisey

Copyright © 2017 Dr. Gus N. Daisey

All rights reserved.

ISBN: 1978197993
ISBN-13: 978-1978197992

DEDICATION

I dedicate this book to all "Deplorables."

Dr. Gus N. Daisey

CONTENTS

1 CHAPTER ONE

God's people fasted, prayed, and voted.

ABOUT THE AUTHOR

Dr. Daisey lives a life full of excitement in the daily crucible of the American work place. He loves God, his wife, and his children. He lives his life to the fullest, knowing that he has been close to death on more than one occasion. He simply tries to love others because God loves him. While many hypotheses have been offered for what happened in the 2016 election for the American president, Dr. Daisey believes that the account in this book is the most accurate.